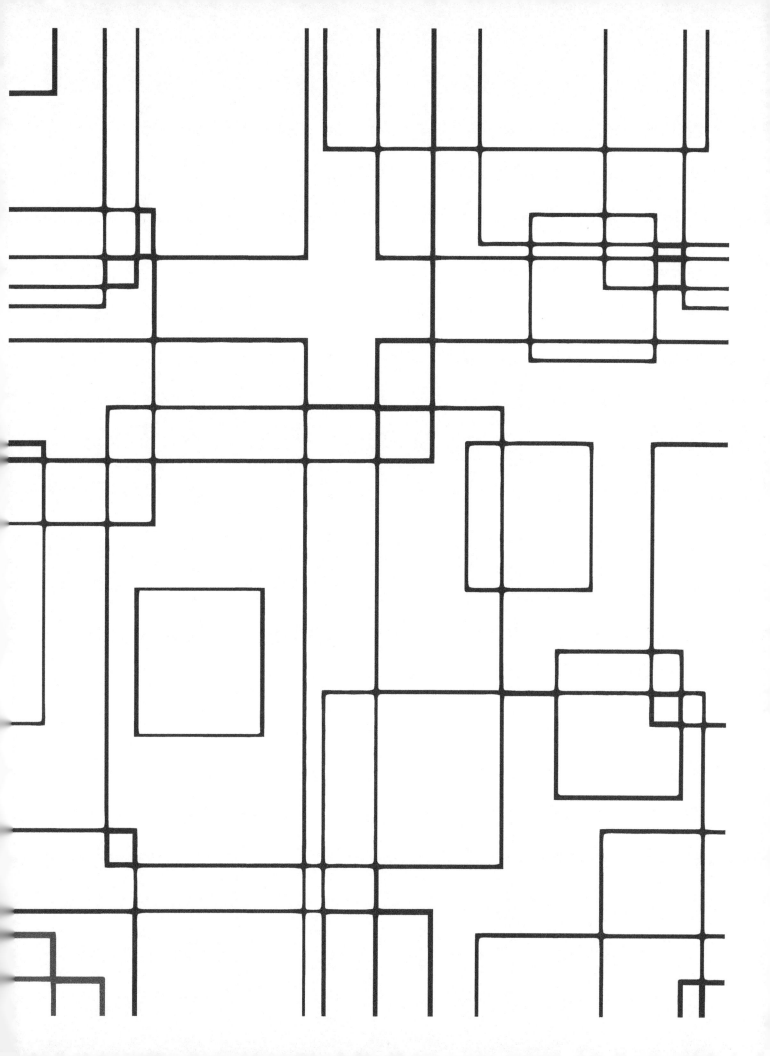

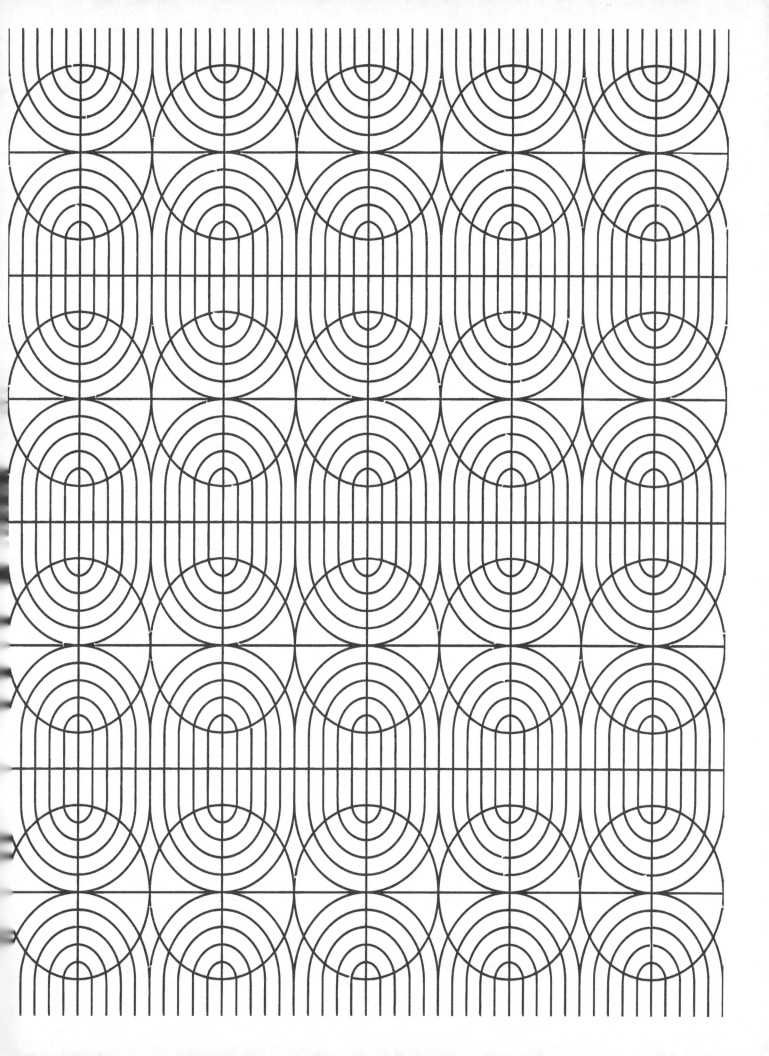

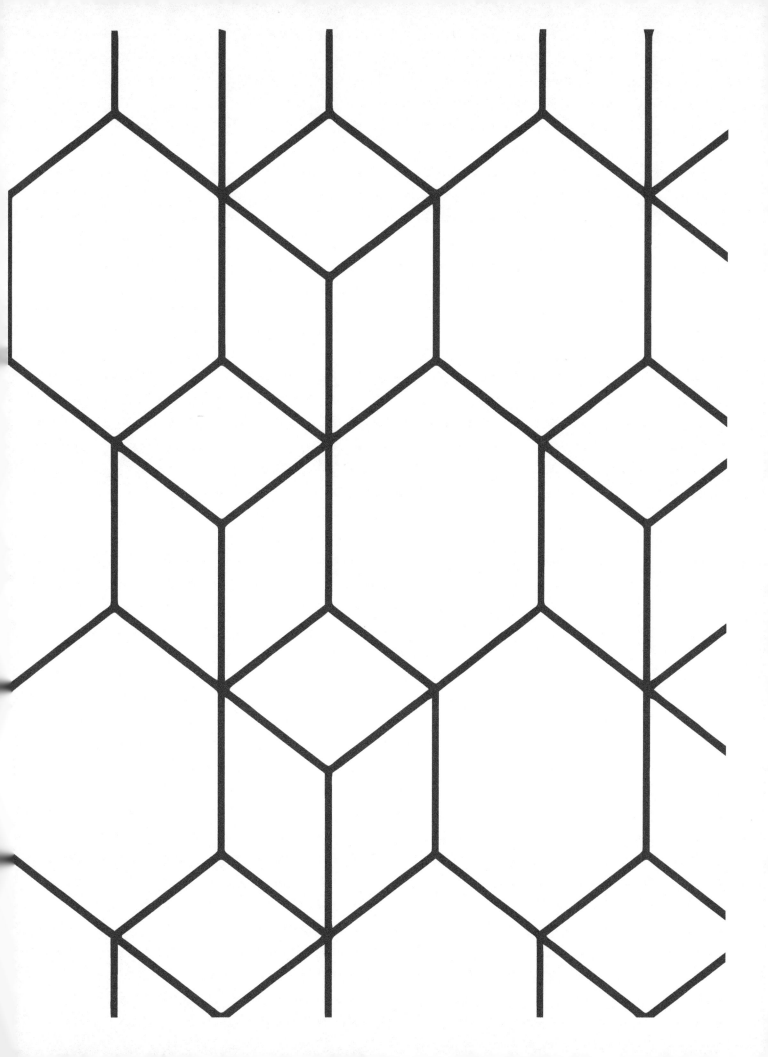

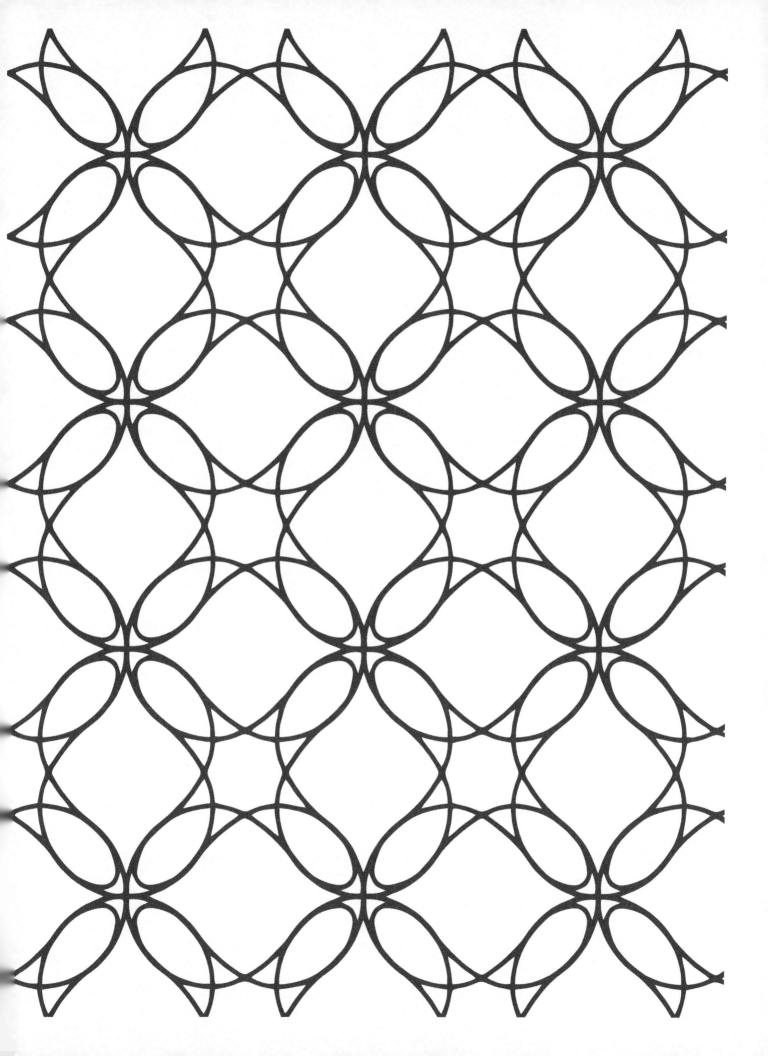

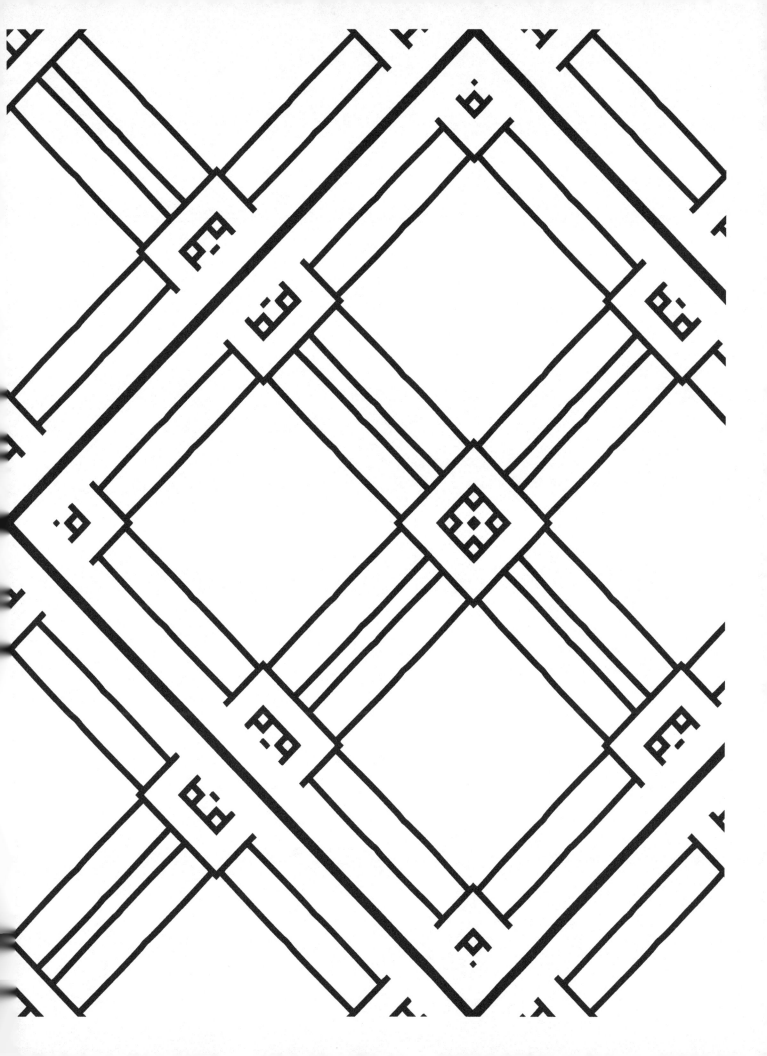

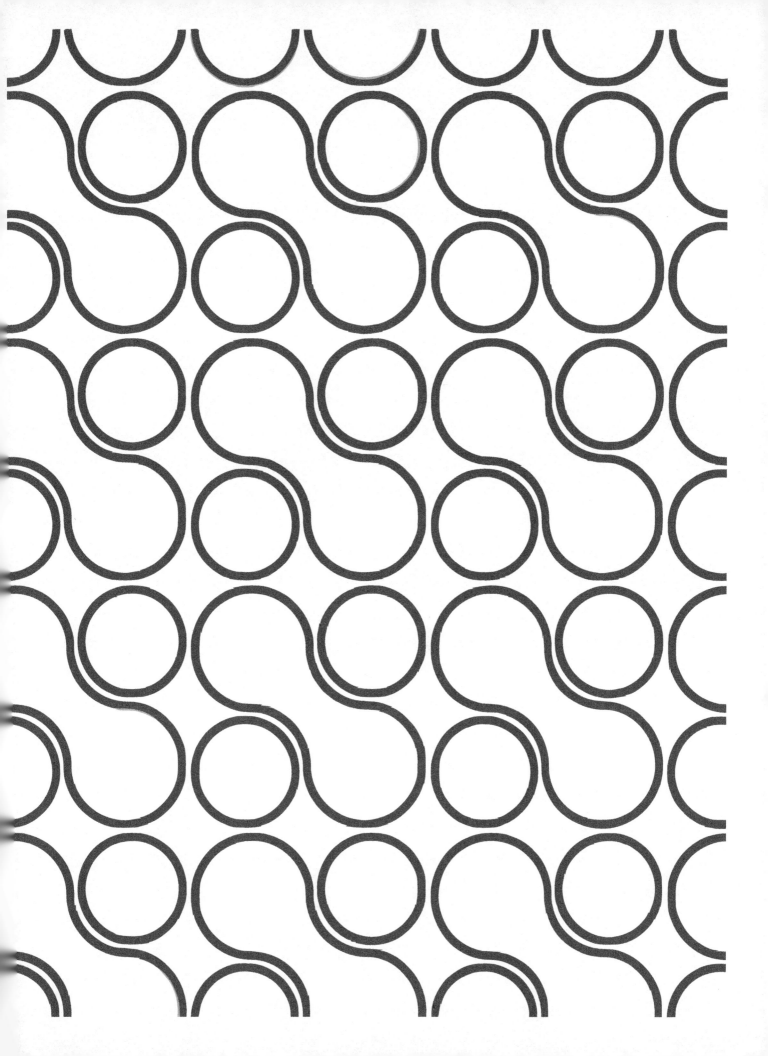

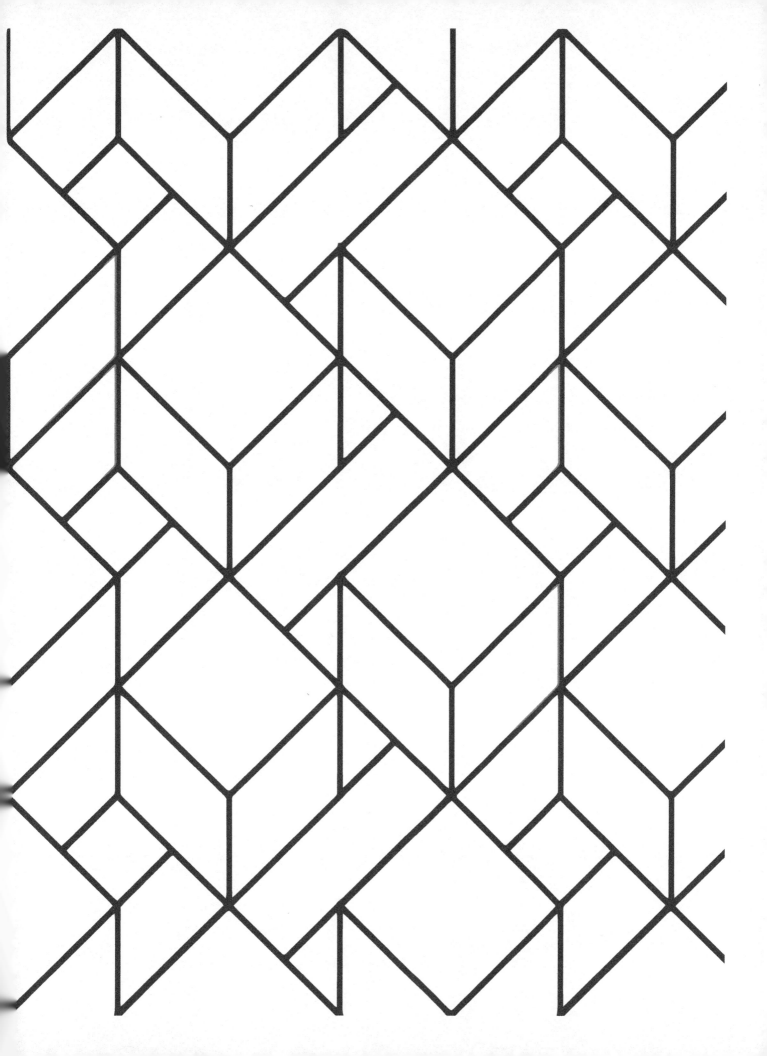

IF YOU LIKED THIS BOOK THEN WE RECOMMEND THAT YOU MIGHT LIKE THIS ONE TOO! PLEASE SCAN THE CODE BELOW

FOR US

FOR UK

IF YOU LIKED THIS BOOK THEN WE RECOMMEND THAT YOU MIGHT LIKE THIS ONE TOO. PLEASE SCAN THE CODE BELOW

FOR US

FOR UK

Made in the USA
Monee, IL
14 May 2025

17423627R00057